Easy To Make And Use

READING BULLETIN BOARDS

With Activities To Supplement Your Daily Reading Program

by
Imogene Forte
and
Mary Ann Pangle

Incentive Publications, Inc.
Nashville, Tennessee

Edited by Jennifer Goodman
Illustrated by Mary Hamilton
Cover by Susan Eaddy

ISBN 0-86530-134-4

Table Of Contents

Preface 5

Between The Bookends — *developing independent reading skills* 7

Button Up! — *putting words in alphabetical order* 8

Character Traits — *understanding and identifying character traits* 9

Clue Sleuths — *building independent reading* 10

Come Fly With Me! — *identifying and using possessives* 11

Compound Cut Outs — *identifying compound words* 12

Consonant Gallery — *discriminating between final consonant sounds* 13

Contraction Cone — *writing contractions* 14

Dig This Dialogue! — *using quotation marks* 16

Drawing Conclusions — *drawing conclusions* 17

Falling For Good Books — *evaluating and summarizing books* 18

Figurative Fireworks — *recognizing and using figures of speech* 19

Figure It Out! — *identifying cause-effect relationships* 20

Go Fly A Kite! — *recognizing consonant sounds* 21

Hot Off The Press — *using the newspaper* 22

Hung-Up On Resources! — *using resource books* 23

Idiom Insights — *using idioms* 24

It's All In Your Head — *visualizing* 25

Just What The Doctor Ordered! — *following written directions* 26

Journey To The Planet Nym — *using antonyms, synonyms and homonyms* 27

Literature Lollipops — *developing reading appreciation* 28

Match-A-Scoop — *recognizing and matching upper and lower case letters* 29

Monkeying Around With Stories — *creating stories from pictures* 30

Newspaper Know-How — *reading the newspaper* 31

Notable Notes — *writing notes in outline form* 32

Opposites Attract — *identifying opposites* 33

The Order Of Things — *ordering ideas in sequence* 34

Perfect Pronunciation — *using the dictionary pronunciation key* 35

Poetry Pin-Ups — *appreciating poetry* 36

Pot Of Plurals — *recognizing and using plurals* 37

Predicting Outcomes — *predicting outcomes* 38

Punctuation Practice — *using punctuation* 39

Read-A-Thon — *using a bar graph* 40

Read To Find Out — *using research materials* 41

Rhyme Race — *identifying rhyming words* 42

"Sign" Language — *recognizing word relationships using picture clues* 43

Sound Match — *using beginning consonant sounds* 44

Sound Off — *recognizing and using beginning sounds* 45

Starring Abbreviations — *recognizing and using abbreviations* 46
Step Up To Better Grades — *improving test performance* 47
Study Sense — *improving study skills* 48
Summary Solutions — *summarizing information* 49
Syllable Salad — *writing words in syllables* 50
Touchdown Teasers! — *distinguishing between fact and opinion* 51
Try Our Alphabet Soup — *recognizing letters* 52
We Love Reading — *developing reading appreciation* 53
We Read And Write Signs — *discriminating visually* 54
What Would They Say? — *using imagery and dialogue* 55
Where In The World? — *reading maps* 56
Windy Words — *recognizing vocabulary words* 57
Word Worms — *using vocabulary words* 58

BULLETIN BOARDS INSTEAD OF BOOK REPORTS 59
Around The World With Books 60
In Your Own Words 60
Puppet Personalities 60
Just Hanging Around 61
Ring Around The Story 61
Character Celebration 61
Going To Pieces 62
Dress It Up 62
Wish You Were Here 62
What A Doll! 63
Riddlerers 63
You Really Hit The Spot! 63

Preface

Teaching kids how to read is a never-ending, all-encompassing task. Teachers use all sorts of methods and styles with all sorts of textbooks, basal readers and supplementary materials to teach all sorts of kids who learn at different rates and in different ways. Sometimes it can be overwhelming. At other times, it can be rewarding and gratifying. Because reading is such an important subject for all ages, it makes sense to use reading themes as a major focus for bulletin boards and other classroom displays. Utilizing bulletin boards to teach reading can help take the drudgery out of reading, stir up motivation, provide some fun and add color and atmosphere to the room.

Classrooms or reading labs which feature colorful, contemporary, motivational and reinforcing bulletin board displays, convey the message to sudents that "this teacher believes reading is important." Teacher-made bulletin boards also affirm the teacher's personal committment to creating a positive and pleasant environment for learning. Because there are many demands made on a teacher's time and energy, this book of bulletin board plans was created expressly to give busy teachers some new ideas to add to their own "tried and true" collection.

This book features over 70 easy-to-make-and-use bulletin boards - all of them complete reading lessons in themselves. In addition to attractively featuring topics of high interest to kids, every board comes complete with skills-based activities to be used right along with adopted textbooks or other reading programs. Each bulletin board is labeled to indicate the specific skills it is designed to teach. A wide variety of skills are covered, offering reading reinforcement all year long. With clear instructions for construction and use, plus suggestions for extending many of the activities, these bulletin boards are quick to create making teaching reading easier for teachers and learning to read more exciting for kids.

SKILL: Developing independent reading skills

CONSTRUCTION
1. Enlarge and reproduce the bulletin board example.
2. Cut large bookends from colorful construction paper and pin to the board or for added interest use real stuffed animals.
3. Make a title strip for the board.
4. Make books from colored construction paper.
5. Provide strips of paper for book reviews and attach to the board.

USE
1. Have students write a brief review of their favorite book on a review strip and sign their name to it.
2. Then ask them to attach the strip to the outside of a construction paper book and, with a felt tip pen, write on it the name of their book and the author.
3. Tell them to pin the book and the review between the bookends as a recommendation to other students.

SKILL: Putting words in alphabetical order

CONSTRUCTION
1. Enlarge and reproduce the bulletin board example.
2. Make the clown coat and buttons from brightly colored construction paper.
3. Make 26 word button covers. Write words beginning with the letters A through Z on them.
4. Put 8 word button covers on the bottom of the board at a time. Change them as often as is appropriate for students' abilities.

USE

Have students pin the word button covers on the coat buttons in alphabetical order.

CHARACTER TRAITS

SKILLS: Understanding and identifying character traits

CONSTRUCTION
1. Enlarge and reproduce the bulletin board example.
2. Decorate the masks with ribbon.
3. Make small mask shapes from colored construction paper for each student.

USE
1. Call attention to the different character traits which the masks on the bulletin board display.
2. Read a story to the class. List the characters' traits on the chalkboard after a group discussion.
3. Ask students to read a book or a story. After completing the book or story, instruct students to take a small mask from the bulletin board, write on it the title of the book or story and then a list of the characters' traits.
4. Display the masks on the bulletin board.
5. Provide time for students to come to the bulletin board, identify their mask and tell about the traits of the characters in their book or story.

SKILL: Building independent reading

CONSTRUCTION
1. Enlarge and reproduce the bulletin board example.
2. Print clues to reading list books on index cards.
3. Place cards on the board.
4. Provide a prize for the winner such as a book, bookmark or extra library time.

USE
1. Ask students to locate the clues by using the reading list books.
2. As they locate the clues, have them write the name of the book, where it was found, author, page number, their name and the date on a piece of paper.
3. At the end of a specified time, the student with the greatest number of answers is declared the winner of the Teacher's Treasure Hunt.

Note:
This is a great warm-up, get acquainted for middle grades back to school activity. It can be used for special topics such as nature, holidays or social studies. For primary grades, the clues should be very simple. (Example: find porcupine, find robin or find zoo. Be sure to give the page number.)

SKILLS: Identifying and using possessives

CONSTRUCTION
1. Enlarge and reproduce the bulletin board example.
2. Make the windows out of brightly colored construction paper.
3. Prepare round activity sheets which contain words, sentences, paragraphs and stories for students to practice using possessives and attach them to the windows of the plane.
4. Prepare a self-checking key.

USE
1. Review possessives by calling attention to the bulletin board.
2. Explain the activity on each plane window. Ask students to take a ride on the Possessive Plane by completing an activity from each window and then evaluating it by using the self-checking key.
3. Provide time to discuss the students' work.

COMPOUND CUT OUTS

sunflower

football

goldfish

birdhouse

snowman

SKILL: Identifying compound words

CONSTRUCTION
1. Enlarge and reproduce the bulletin board example.
2. Magazine pictures may be used instead of the illustrations provided.
3. Provide construction paper, markers and scissors.

USE
1. Ask students to draw, color, label and cut out, pictures which illustrate compound words.
2. Allow students to share their pictures and add them to the bulletin board.
3. Review compound words by calling attention to the compound words and pictures on the bulletin board.

CONSONANT GALLERY

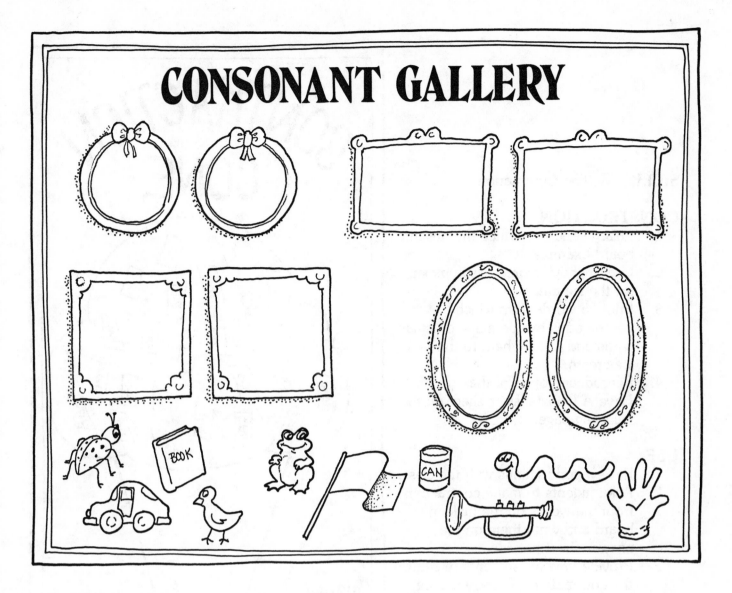

SKILL: Discriminating between final consonant sounds

CONSTRUCTION
1. Enlarge and reproduce the bulletin board example.
2. Make several pairs of matching frames from construction paper or wrapping paper.
3. Provide many pairs of pictures with like final consonant sounds.

USE
1. Have the students pin the pictures with like final consonant sounds in matching frames.
2. Change the pictures often to provide practice with many more final consonants.

   Optional:
   Have the students make a list of other words with like final consonants.

SKILL: Writing Contractions

CONSTRUCTION

1. Enlarge and reproduce the bulletin board example.
2. Use brightly colored tissue paper for the ice cream.
3. Print 25 words from which contractions can be made on small cards and attach them to the ice cream.
4. Reproduce copies of the Have A Cone answer sheet on the following page.

USE

1. Review contractions with the class.
2. Ask students to make contractions from the words on the bulletin board and write them on the answer sheet provided.
3. Provide time for students to share the contractions. Display the ice cream cone answer shapes on the bulletin board.

Note: This activity may be used during reading group time.

14

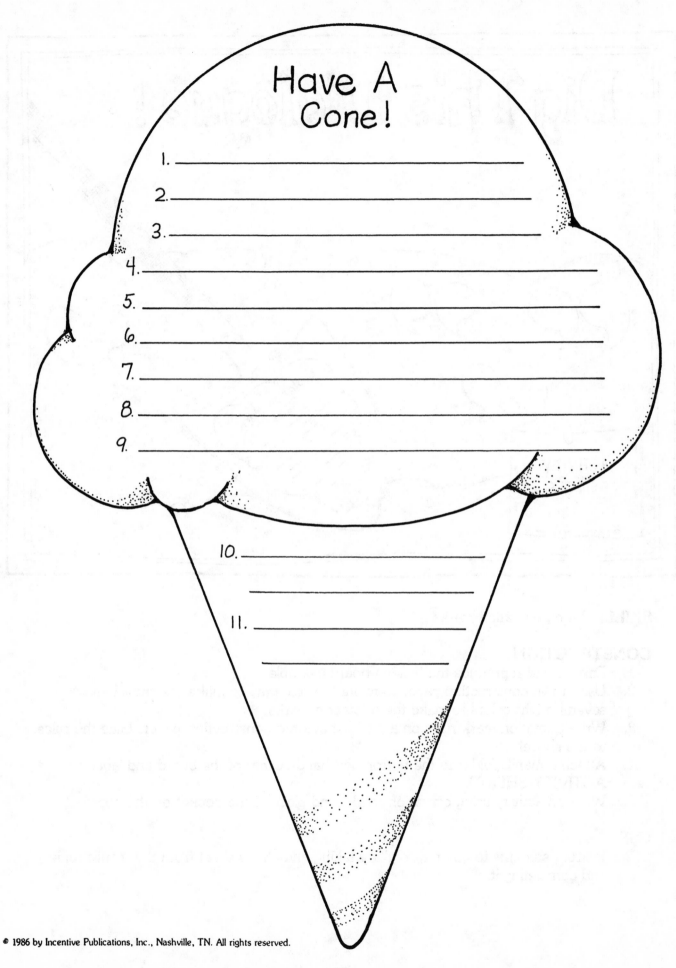

Have A Cone!

1. _____

2. _____

3. _____

4. _____

5. _____

6. _____

7. _____

8. _____

9. _____

10. _____

_____

11. _____

_____

SKILL: Using quotation marks

CONSTRUCTION
1. Enlarge and reproduce the bulletin board example.
2. Use brown construction paper to make the soil, gray to make the shovel and several bright colors to make the quotation marks.
3. Write quotation mark rules on a piece of colored construction paper. Glue the rules to the shovel.
4. Attach a manila folder to the bottom left hand corner of the board and label it ACTIVITY SHEETS.
5. Write an activity using quotation marks and place in the pocket on the board.

USE
Instruct students to go on a "dig" by taking an activity sheet from the manila folder and completing it.

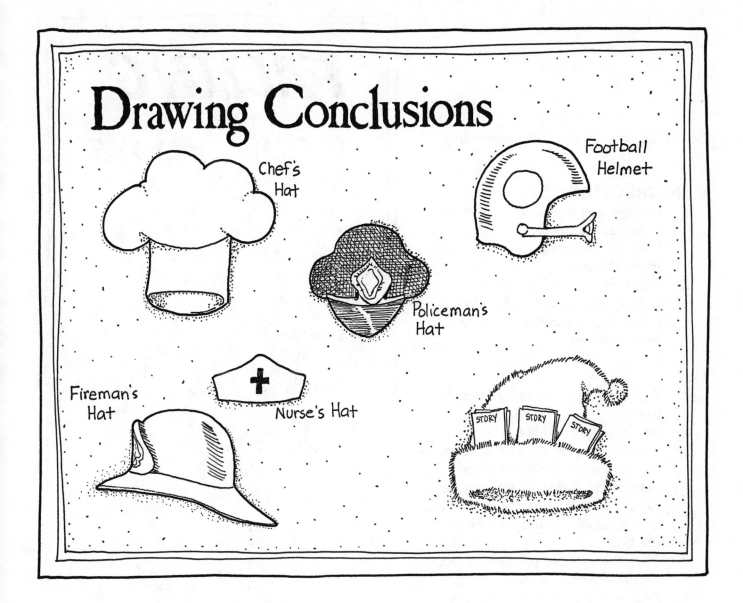

Drawing Conclusions

Chef's Hat

Football Helmet

Policeman's Hat

Fireman's Hat

Nurse's Hat

STORY STORY STORY

SKILL: Drawing conclusions

CONSTRUCTION
1. Enlarge and reproduce the bulletin board example.
2. Use real hats if they are available or let students design the hats.
3. Use textured, colorful and patterned materials to make the hats.

USE
1. Discuss the uses of hats. (Example: safety, identity, etc.)
2. Cut out paragraphs or stories from old reading books, workbooks, newspapers and comic strips. Make a pocket in the stocking cap and insert them. During reading group, let the students read a story and write their conclusions.
3. Provide time for follow up.

SKILLS: Evaluating and summarizing books

CONSTRUCTION
1. Enlarge and reproduce the bulletin board example.
2. Use brown construction paper to make the tree.
3. Make the leaves from green, yellow, orange, red and brown construction paper and pin to the tree branches.

USE
1. Assign several books for students to read.
2. As students complete a book, instruct them to take a leaf from the tree and write the name of the author and their name on one side. On the other side, have them write a brief summary and evaluation of the book.
3. Then tell them to pin the leaf back on the board as a Falling Leaf.
4. After a period of time, students who have read the same book may compare notes and share them with the class.

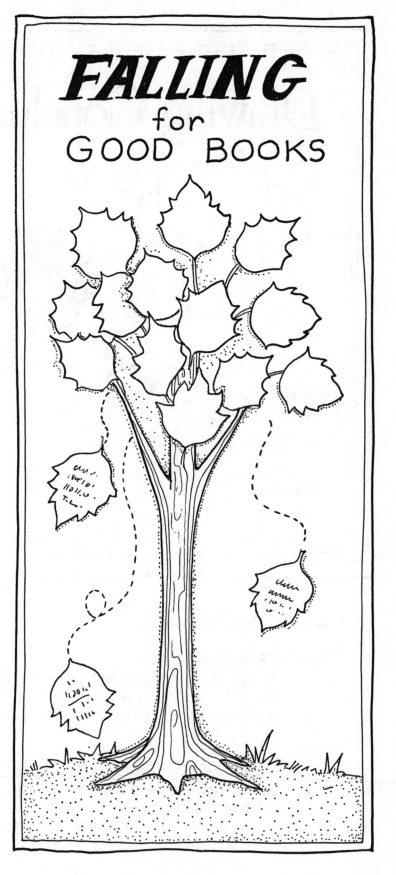

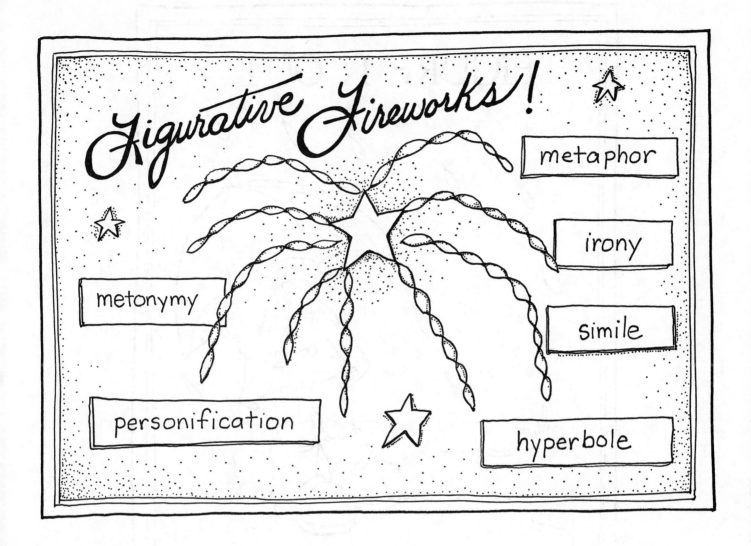

SKILLS: Recognizing and using figures of speech

CONSTRUCTION
1. Enlarge and reproduce the bulletin board example.
2. Cover the board with black construction paper.
3. Twist strips of brightly colored crepe paper and attach them to the board to resemble fireworks.
4. Print the following words on pieces of construction paper and attach to the bulletin board: similes, metaphors, irony, metonymy, hyperbole and personification.

USE
1. Use the bulletin board as a review or an introduction to figures of speech.
2. Plan a Figure of Speech Week. Involve your students each day in a creative writing project. (Example: poems, stories, slogans or cartoons.) Each project must include at least 2 different figures of speech until all figures of speech have been used. On the last day, ask everyone to write a story using all the figures of speech.
3. For added reinforcement, instruct the students to choose a partner, exchange papers and identify figures of speech in their partner's writing.

FIGURE IT OUT

SKILL: Identifying cause-effect relationships

CONSTRUCTION
1. Enlarge and reproduce the bulletin board example.
2. Use brightly colored construction paper for the umbrella and raincoat.

USE
1. Ask students to identify the cause and effect relationship shown on the bulletin board.
2. Provide examples of cause-effect relationships from old reading workbooks or prepare new ones. Attach these to the bulletin board.
3. Allow time for students to take and complete an activity by writing the cause and effect relationship for each one.
4. Provide time for students to share their answers.

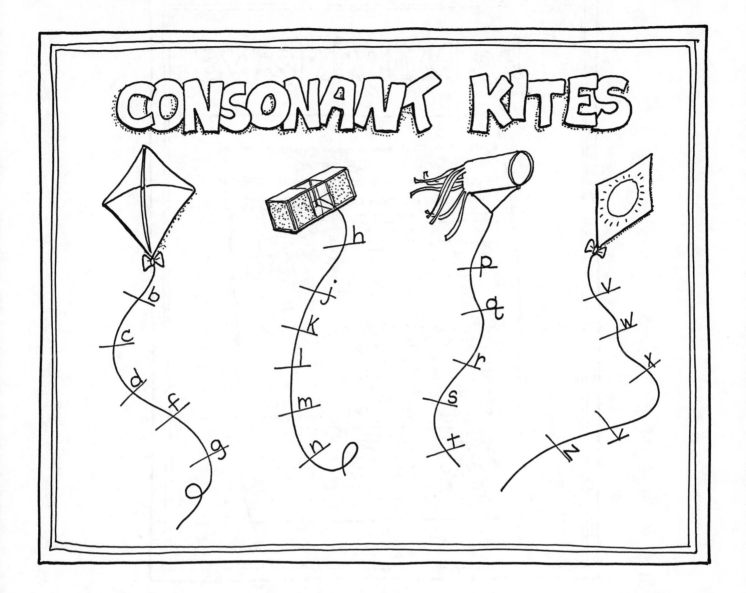

SKILL: Recognizing consonant sounds

CONSTRUCTION
1. Enlarge and reproduce the bulletin board example.
2. Use gift-wrap paper to make 4 kites.
3. Make kite tails out of crepe or tissue paper.
4. Print consonants on each tail as shown.

USE
1. Use this bulletin board as a review of consonants.
2. Ask each student to come to the board, point to a consonant, say the consonant sound and give a word which begins or ends with that consonant.

SKILL: Using the newspaper

CONSTRUCTION
Enlarge and reproduce the bulletin board example.

USE
1. Use the bulletin board as enrichment and reinforcement while teaching a unit on the newspaper.
2. Plan a field trip to see how a newspaper is written and published.
3. Let the class write their own newspaper. Divide the students into small groups. Ask each group to write an article. You may want to assign a topic to each group such as sports, current events, lifestyes, entertainment, etc. Take each group through the steps of writing, editing, proofing, rewriting and layout. Display one section of the class newspaper each day on the bulletin board.

SKILL: Using resource books

CONSTRUCTION
1. Enlarge and reproduce the bulletin board example.
2. Make cars from different colors of posterboard.
3. Attach the cars with colored yarn.
4. Provide examples of each kind of resource book on a table near the bulletin board.
5. Prepare a list of topics for students to research.

USE
1. Discuss the different resources available for research by pointing to each word on the bulletin board.
2. Divide the class into small groups. Give each group one example of a resource. Ask students to suggest topics for further research. Then let each group use the resource to find facts on the subject. Provide time for students to share the data and resource.
3. Give each student a topic to research. Ask the students to use several different resources, take notes on the topic and list the resources used.

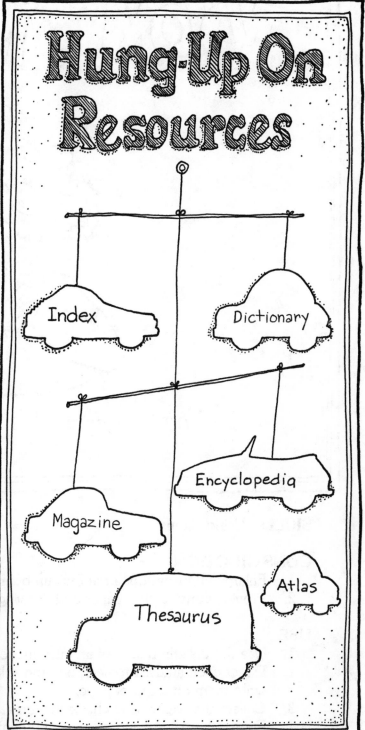

"The singer had a frog in her throat".

SKILL: Using idioms

CONSTRUCTION
1. Enlarge and reproduce the bulletin board example.
2. Provide construction paper and drawing materials for the students.

USE
1. Use the bulletin board as an introduction for a discussion of idioms.
2. Direct each student to seek out and select three favorite idiomatic expressions and write them on a slip of paper.
3. Collect the papers and check two on each sheet, screening out all doubles.
4. Return the papers and ask each student to create a page for a class booklet by humorously illustrating the chosen two idioms. (One on the front and one on the back.)
5. Collect all pages and bind them together to form a book of idioms for the students to enjoy.

SKILL: Visualizing

CONSTRUCTION
1. Enlarge and reproduce the bulletin board example.
2. Use wrapping paper to make the magic bottle.
3. Use glitter for magic potion coming out of bottle.

USE
1. Ask the class to think about what the girl on the board might be visualizing. Have them write a story about it.
2. Read a story to the class. Ask them to visualize the scenes and action in the story and then illustrate it on drawing paper like a film.
3. Change the picture on the bulletin board to show the girl visualizing something different. Again, ask the class to write a story about it. Note: This can be done several times.

SKILL: Following written directions

CONSTRUCTION

1. Enlarge and reproduce the bulletin board example.
2. Cover the board with brightly colored construction paper.
3. Use light blue, grey or light pink for the bottle and white paper for the directions.

USE

1. Call attention to the bulletin board and let the students enjoy the message which is written on it.
2. Ask students to write their own directions for a fictitious medicine. Provide time for students to share their directions. Display them on or near the bulletin board.

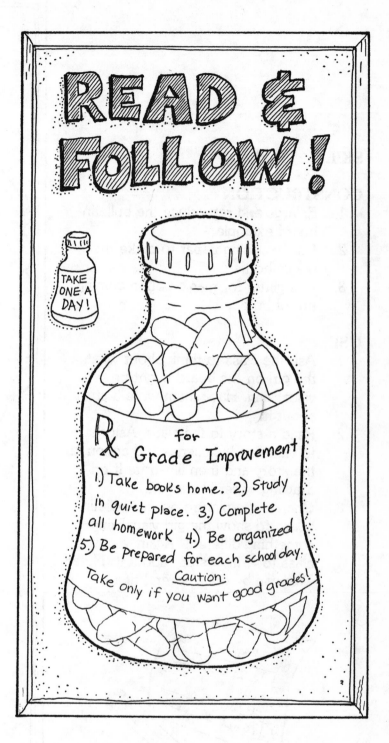

SKILLS: Using antonyms, synonyms, and homonyms

CONSTRUCTION
1. Enlarge and reproduce the bulletin board example.
2. Clouds should be designed as pockets to hold the cards.
3. Provide drawing paper for students to make their own rockets.
4. On index cards, print words that have an antonym, synonym or homonym and place them behind the related cloud.
5. Make an answer key.

USE
1. Instruct students to blast off into space on the rockets they have made, by taking a journey to the planet Nym. On the way to Nym, they must stop at each cloud, take a word card and write the corresponding antonym, homonym or synonym on their rocket.
2. Use the answer key to check answers.
3. Send the completed rocket to Nym by attaching it to the bulletin board.

SKILL: Developing reading appreciation

CONSTRUCTION
1. Enlarge and reproduce the bulletin board example.
2. Use brightly colored paper to make the lollipops.
3. Make the title out of dark or bright paper.

USE
1. Use the board to stimulate class discussions on literature categories.
2. Ask students to select and read a book from one of the literature categories.
3. Ask the students to make their own lollipop each time they read a book, writing on it the name of the book read, the literature category and their name.
4. Then let them put their lollipops on the board underneath the correct literature category.

28

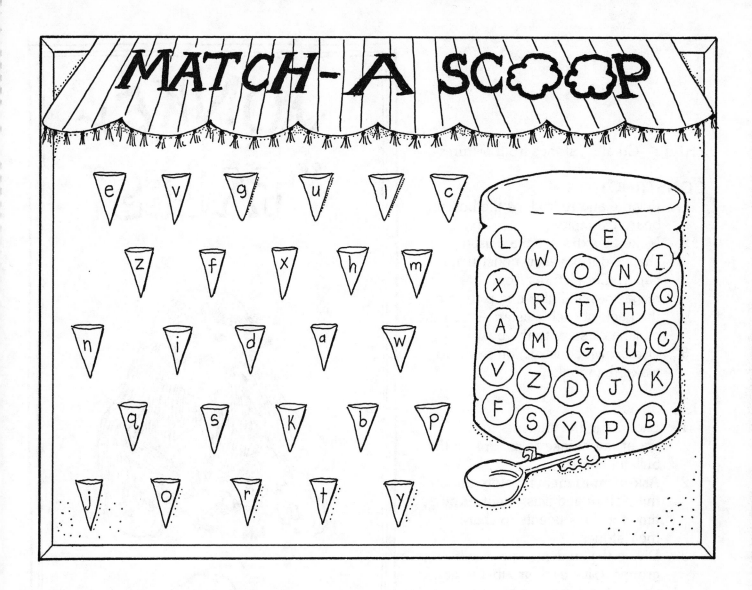

SKILLS: Recognizing and matching upper and lower case letters

CONSTRUCTION
1. Enlarge and reproduce the bulletin board example.
2. Cut ice cream cones from manila or light brown construction paper and ice cream dips from a contrasting color.
3. Print lower case letters on the cones and upper case letters on the dips.

USE

Ask students to match upper and lower case letters by pinning the ice cream dip on the ice cream cone.

Optional:
Ask students to order the cones alphabetically.

SKILL: Creating stories from pictures

CONSTRUCTION
1. Enlarge and reproduce the bulletin board example.
2. Make 20 extra banana cluster shapes out of yellow construction paper. Cut pictures from magazines and glue one picture on the back of each cluster. Attach the banana clusters to the board.
3. Use brown construction paper to make the monkey.

USE
1. Encourage the students to talk about the monkey's picture on the bulletin board.
2. Ask them to create a story about the picture and illustrate it. Provide time for the students to share their stories.
3. Divide the students into small groups. Give each group a large sheet of paper and a banana cluster. Instruct them to create a story about the picture on the back of the cluster and write it down. Provide time for the group to share their stories.

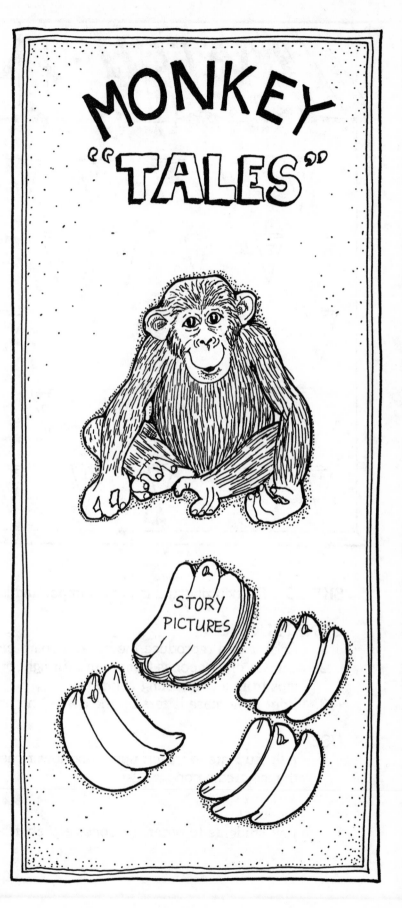

Newspaper Know-How

SKILL: Reading the newspaper

CONSTRUCTION
1. Enlarge and reproduce the bulletin board example.
2. Cut the large, background shapes out of colorful construction paper and attach them to the board.

USE

Have students bring news articles, headlines, cartoons, ads, editorials, etc. to school. Attach the articles to the large shapes on the board.

Optional:
- If possible, have the daily newspaper delivered to the classroom. Place it on a reading table near the board.
- Or, for added reinforcement, ask the kids to bring as many different kinds of newspapers to class as possible for show and tell and later display. (Example: school, daily, Sunday, church, club, foreign, etc.)

SKILL: Writing notes in outline form

CONSTRUCTION
1. Enlarge and reproduce the bulletin board example.
2. Cut music note shapes from black construction paper.

USE
1. Introduce the skill of writing notes in outline form by using the bulletin board example. Complete the outline with the students' participation.
2. Divide the class into small groups. Assign a topic for each group to research. Ask each group to write notes on their favorite topic in outline form following the outline given.
3. For added reinforcement, provide time for each group to present and explain their outline.

SKILL: Identifying opposites

CONSTRUCTION

1. Enlarge and reproduce the bulletin board example.
2. Paint faces on white tagboard or make faces out of construction paper.
3. Use orange paper for the hair and bright fabric for collars.

USE

1. Introduce or review opposite words.
2. Read a word and ask students to write down an opposite word.
3. Ask students to write lists of opposite words.
4. Have them illustrate some of their opposite words.

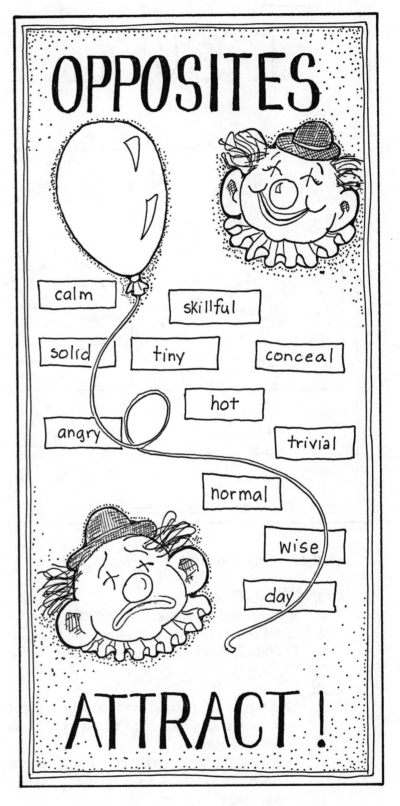

The Order of Things

1 2 3

SKILL: Ordering ideas in sequence

CONSTRUCTION
1. Enlarge and reproduce the bulletin board example.
2. Use brown construction paper for the nests, red for the birds and white for the egg.
3. Do not attach birds and nest figures to the board.

USE
1. Use the bulletin board for teaching sequence.
2. Ask individual students to come to the bulletin board and arrange the pictures in correct sequence.
3. Ask students to illustrate other ideas in sequence to share with the class. (Example: dressing for school, eating breakfast, visiting the doctor, making a cake, bathing a dog, etc.)

Say It Like It Is

Kăsh (cache)

shēk (chic)

ə trib'yōot (attribute)

gāj (gauge)

sīth (scythe)

SKILL: Using the dictionary pronunciation key.

CONSTRUCTION
1. Enlarge and reproduce the bulletin board example.
2. Use red and pink construction paper for the mouths.

USE
1. Review the pronunciation key in a dictionary or basal reader.
2. Demonstrate the use of the key to pronounce words listed on the bulletin board.
3. For added reinforcement, say a word and ask the class to look up the correct pronunciation. This can be done orally or in writing.

SKILL: Appreciating poetry

CONSTRUCTION

1. Designate one bulletin board as the poetry pin-up board.
2. Select a student committee for each week to be responsible for the board. The committee will determine what type of poetry is to be displayed during the week, create a title for the board, be responsible for arranging the display and judging the best entry at the end of the week.

USE

1. Students select a poem in the given category, copy and illustrate it as they see fit.
2. The blue ribbon entry will be judged on appropriateness of the poem selected, neatness and originality of presentation and illustrations.
3. Categories that might be used include: poems written by kids, nature poems, poems about the weather, poems written by American writers, big city poems, poems about animals, nighttime poems, poems with a fantasy theme and Mother Goose rhymes.

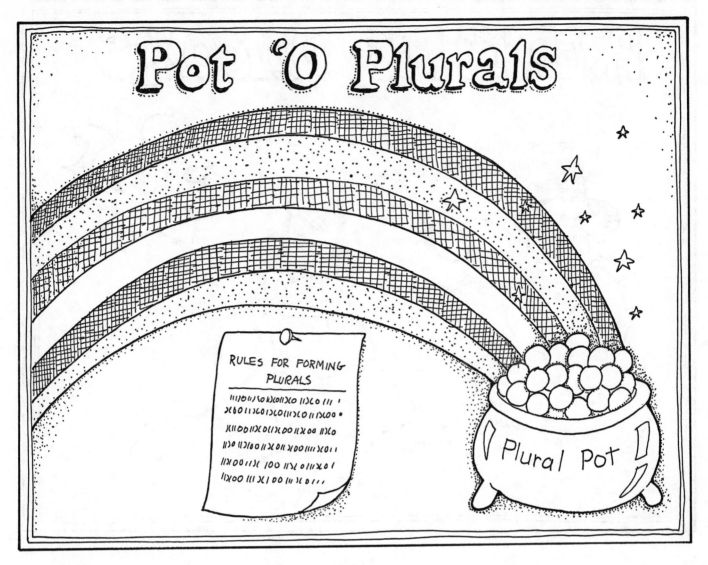

SKILLS: Recognizing and using plurals

CONSTRUCTION
1. Enlarge and reproduce the bulletin board example.
2. Cut strips of tissue paper for the rainbow from each of the following colors: violet, blue, green, yellow, orange and red.
3. Make 20 gold coins from gold paper.
4. Print words from which plurals can be made on the coins and attach them to the bulletin board.

USE
1. Review the rules for forming plurals. Write a word to illustrate each rule on the board.
2. Divide the students into two teams. Tell the first two players from each team to go to the chalkboard. Read a word on one of the coins. Each player must write the correct plural of that word on the board. The first player to write the correct plural gets one point. Play continues until one team receives a predetermined number of points.

SKILL: Predicting outcomes

CONSTRUCTION
1. Enlarge and reproduce the bulletin board example.
2. Use black construction paper for the hats and red for the scarves.

USE
1. Review predicting by calling attention to the bulletin board.
2. Read a story and lead a discussion on the students' outcome predictions.
3. Follow up on another day by reading part of a story and asking students to draw a picture to show what they think will happen next.
4. Display the pictures on or near the board so the students can enjoy each others' predictions before reading the rest of the story.

SKILL: Using punctuation

CONSTRUCTION
1. Enlarge and reproduce the bulletin board example
2. Make each balloon a different color.
3. Let the kids decorate and create balloon shapes.
4. Use yarn for balloon strings.

USE
1. Read a sentence. Then ask students to come to the board and point to the correct punctuation mark.
2. Have the students make up a paragraph using all the punctuation marks given.
3. Ask them to identify punctuation marks while reading during reading groups. Discuss reasons for punctuation.
4. Prepare punctuation activity sheets by writing sentences and leaving off punctuation. Attach them to one of the balloons on the board. Ask students to complete the activity sheet.

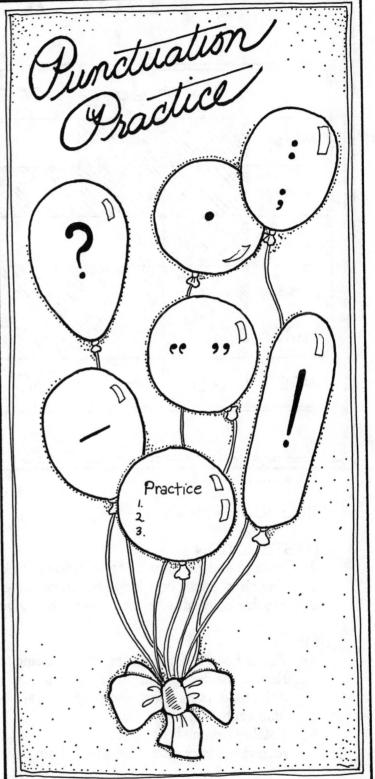

39

READ ~ A ~ THON

Reading Enrichment

	20	40	60	80	100	120
Monday	▨	▨				
Tuesday	▨	▨	▨			
Wednesday	▨					
Thursday	▨	▨	▨	▨	▨	
Friday	▨	▨	▨	▨		
PAGES	20	40	60	80	100	120

SKILL: Using a bar graph

CONSTRUCTION
1. Enlarge and reproduce the bulletin board example.
2. Use chart paper or a long section of white butcher paper for the graph.
3. Provide colored felt markers and library books.

USE
1. Plan a Read-A-Thon to stimulate reading for enjoyment.
2. Review making and using bar graphs with students.
3. Ask students to select and read a library book and then record the number of pages read each day.
4. Total the number of pages read by all students each day. Ask individual students to record the information on the bulletin board graph using the felt tip pens.

Optional:
Make individual bar graph worksheets for each student to record personal reading.

SKILL: Using research materials

CONSTRUCTION
1. Enlarge and reproduce the bulletin board example.
2. Write thought provoking questions, whose answers can be found in library or resource books, on large question marks.
3. Place the question marks in a pocket on the bulletin board.

USE
1. Have the students take a question mark from the board and find answers to the questions.
2. Then have them give the full name, author, date and publisher of the book where the answer was found.

Sample Questions:
1. Did Betsy Ross really make the first flag of the United States? If so, when, where and why? If not, who did, when, where and why?
2. Where is the largest bridge in the world located? When and why was it built? What is the main material used in its construction?
3. What is the largest ocean going vessel in use in the world today? Between what countries does it sail? What is the chief cargo? Who owns it? How old is it?

SKILL: Identifying rhyming words

CONSTRUCTION
1. Enlarge and reproduce the bulletin board example.
2. Use a different color of paper for each shape.
3. Use yellow paper for the lights around each shape.
4. Print one of the following words on six index cards: sit, boat, mop, pail, hat and man. Tape one card on the back of each hexagon shape. (These may be changed daily or weekly.)

USE
1. Review rhyming words.
2. Use the bulletin board to play Rhyme Race. Divide the students into two teams. Turn over one of the hexagon shapes so that the card with the word written on it can be seen. At a given signal, have the students on each team write rhyming words for the word shown. The team who writes the most rhyming words receives one point. Play continues until all of the words behind the hexagon shapes have been used. The team with the most points wins the race.

SKILL: Recognizing word relationships using picture clues

CONSTRUCTION
1. Enlarge and reproduce the bulletin board example.
2. Use red paper for the stop sign, green for the exit sign, white for the bus stop sign, yellow for the no smoking sign and black for the paper doll shapes.

USE
1. Discuss how each shape on the board can be used as a picture clue.
2. Instruct students to make other examples of picture clues. Display them on the bulletin board.

SKILL: Using beginning consonant sounds

CONSTRUCTION
1. Enlarge and reproduce the bulletin board example.
2. Make picture cards by drawing pictures on construction paper or cut out pictures from magazines.
3. Attach yarn to each card with a pin.
4. Make consonant letters for the right side of the board out of black construction paper.
5. Provide pins for the students to use.

USE
1. Attach the free end of each piece of yarn to the correct matching beginning consonant.
2. Change the sounds and pictures at intervals to keep the activity fresh. Extra pictures that could be used: dog, clown, top, kite, or bicycle.

SKILLS: Recognizing and using beginning sounds

CONSTRUCTION
1. Enlarge and reproduce the bulletin board example.
2. Make the Sound Off Ball, at the bottom of the bulletin board, a pocket so that small ball shapes can be inserted.
3. Cut twenty ball shapes from colored construction paper. Paste pictures from magazines on each one. Place the balls in the pocket of the Sound Off Ball.

USE
1. Call attention to the pictures on the bulletin board. Ask students to say the beginning sound of each picture.
2. Divide the students into two teams and play Sound Off.
   Rules:
   - The teacher selects a picture from the Sound Off pocket.
   - The players on each team must say the beginning sound of the picture.
   - The first player to say the correct beginning sound of the picture, receives one point for his/her team.
   - Play continues until one team receives ten points.

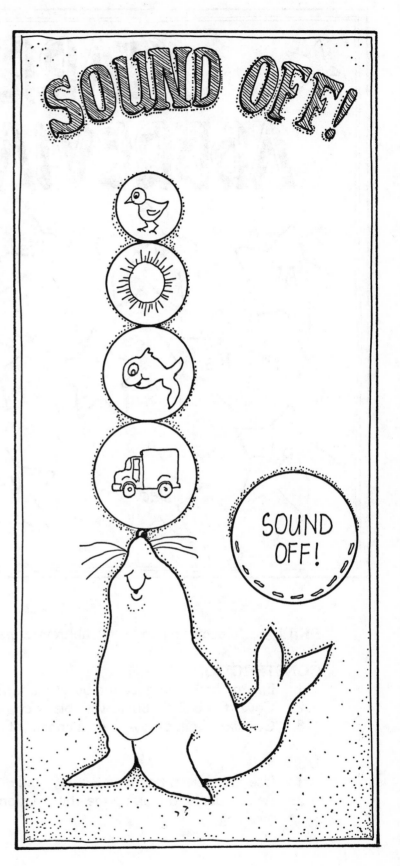

45

SKILLS: Recognizing and using abbreviations

CONSTRUCTION
1. Enlarge and reproduce the bulletin board example.
2. Cover the bulletin board with black construction paper.
3. Cut stars from yellow or gold construction paper.

USE
1. Use the bulletin board as a study guide while teaching abbreviations.
2. Ask students to look up the abbreviations in the dictionary to determine their meaning.

SKILL: Improving test performance

CONSTRUCTION
1. Enlarge and reproduce the bulletin board example.
2. Use bulletin board border paper for the ladder.

USE
1. Introduce the bulletin board before a test is given at the beginning of the year to improve students' test performance.
2. Go over each Test Tip and provide time for students to discuss each item.
3. Continue to use the bulletin board for a period of time to motivate students to improve their test performance.

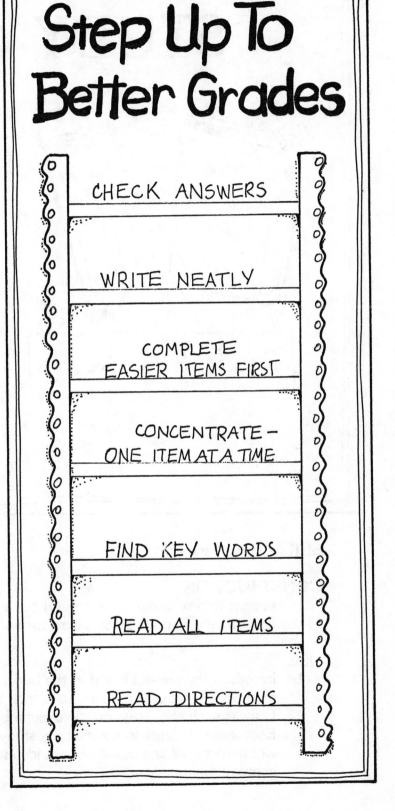

Step Up To Better Grades

CHECK ANSWERS

WRITE NEATLY

COMPLETE EASIER ITEMS FIRST

CONCENTRATE - ONE ITEM AT A TIME

FIND KEY WORDS

READ ALL ITEMS

READ DIRECTIONS

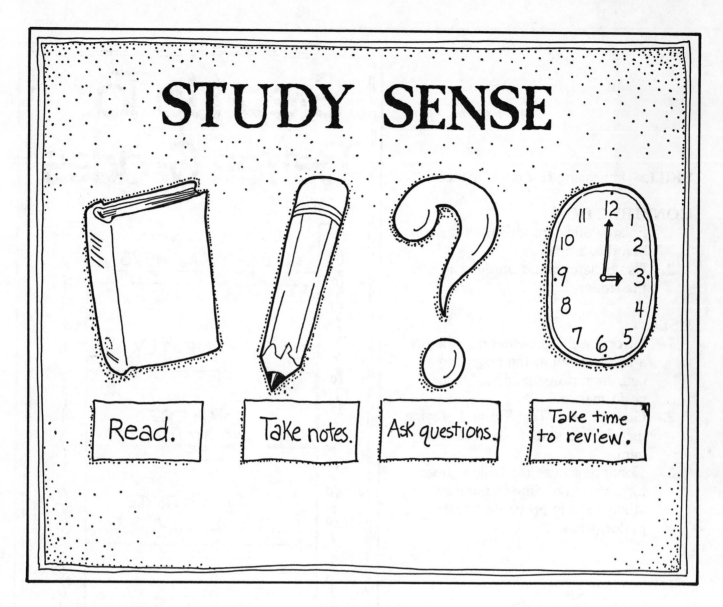

SKILL: Improving study skills

CONSTRUCTION
1. Enlarge and reproduce the bulletin board example.
2. Use brightly colored poster board for each shape.

USE
1. Introduce the bulletin board at the beginning of school or before test time as motivation for students to improve their study skills.
2. Discuss each step listed on the bulletin board.
3. Encourage students to practice the study skills in all areas of the curriculum.
4. Continue to use the bulletin board idea for a period of time to remind students to improve their study skills.

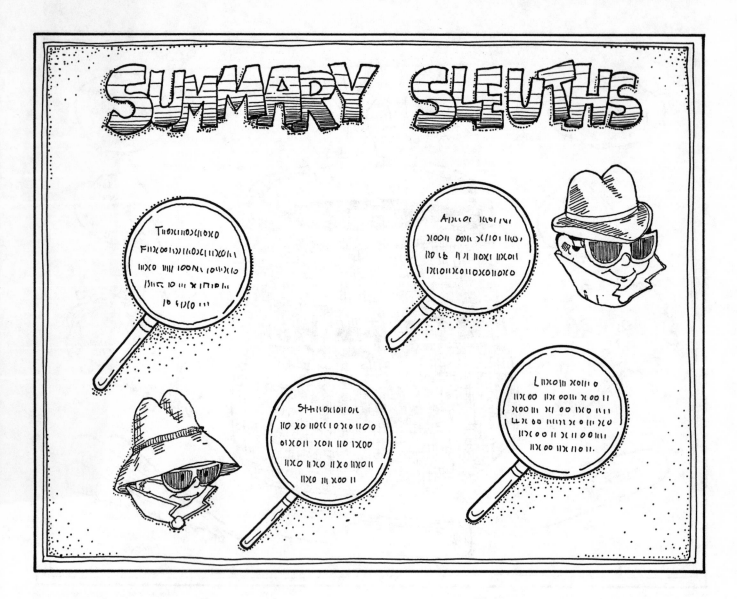

SKILL: Summarizing information

CONSTRUCTION
1. Enlarge and reproduce the bulletin board example.
2. Cut 4 large and 20 small magnifying glass shapes from white poster board.
3. Print an example of a summary on each large magnifyng glass.
4. Cover the large magnifying glass shapes with colored celophane.
5. Cut stories and other types of written information from reading workbooks and paste them on pieces of colored construction paper. Place them near the bulletin board along with the small magnifying glass shapes.

USE
1. Read the stories or other information from which the summaries have been written. Afterwords, ask individual students to come to the bulletin board and read the summary of what was read.
2. Ask students to take a story from the table, read it, and summarize it on one of the small magnifying glass shapes.
3. Provide time for students to share the summaries and display them on the bulletin board.

SKILL: Writing words in syllables

CONSTRUCTION
1. Enlarge and reproduce the bulletin board example.
2. Use brown or black construction paper for the kettle, green for the zucchini, broccoli and celery, red for the tomato and onion, orange for the carrots, brown for the chicken and potato and yellow for the noodles.

USE
1. Introduce the bulletin board by asking students to name ingredients in vegetable soup. As items are named, place them in the soup kettle. Instruct students to write the words in syllables at their desks.
2. Ask students to draw and color six pictures. Let them exchange pictures and then write the names of the pictures in syllables. Provide time for students to share their work. Display pictures and words on or near the bulletin board.

SKILL: Developing reading appreciation

CONSTRUCTION
1. Enlarge and reproduce the bulletin board example.
2. Attach the title to the bulletin board.
3. Provide drawing paper and crayons or tempera paint.

USE
1. Have the students create a bumper sticker to advertise reading library books using drawing paper and crayons or paint.
2. Display the bumper stickers on the bulletin board, on the wall near the board or in the hall.

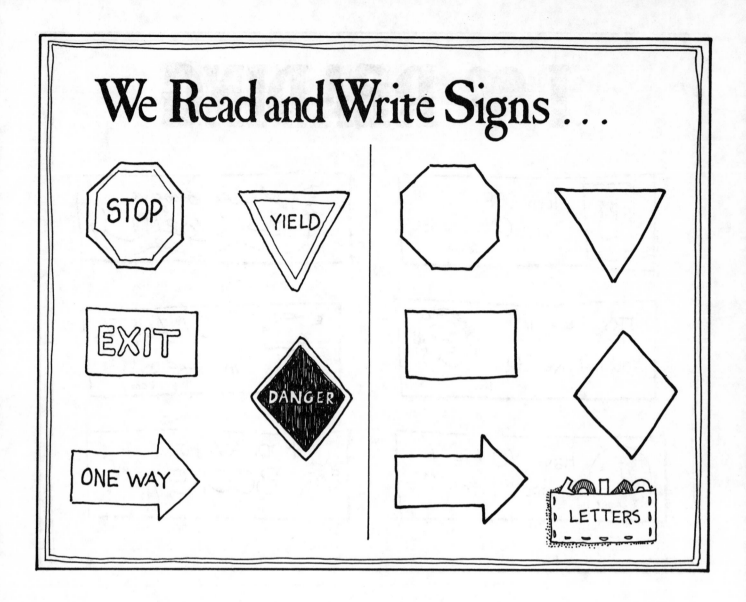

We Read and Write Signs . . .

SKILL: Discriminating visually

CONSTRUCTION
1. Enlarge and reproduce the bulletin board example by creating familiar signs which children can identify with out of cut paper, product packaging or magazine ads.
2. Place these on one side of the bulletin board. On the opposite side, draw an outline of the original sign.
3. Provide letters and other materials in sufficient quantity to recreate the signs.
4. Attach the letters to the bulletin board in a box or envelope.
5. Divide the class into pairs.

USE
1. Ask students to recreate the signs using the loose letters.
2. Instruct partners to check to see if signs are matched correctly letter for letter.
3. Return letters to the box or envelope.

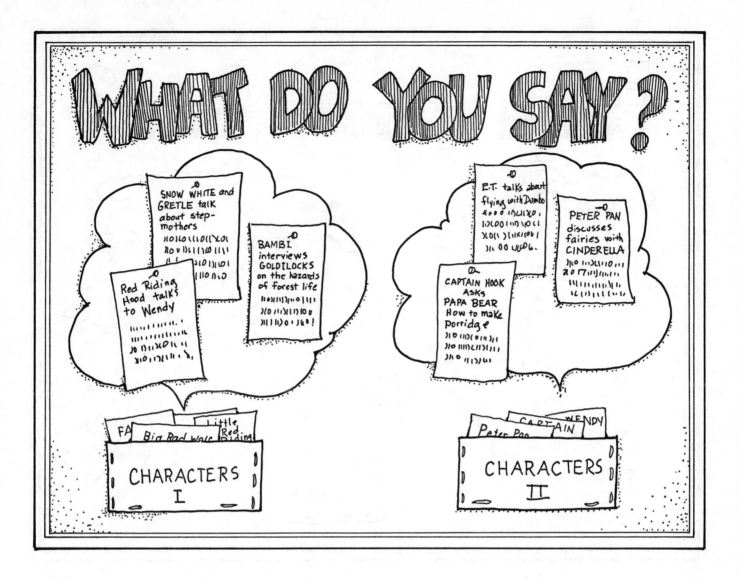

SKILLS: Using imagery and dialogue

CONSTRUCTION
1. Enlarge and reproduce the bulletin board example.
2. Print the names of well known story or book characters on strips of tagboard or index cards. (Example: Snow White, Tom Thumb, E.T., Alice in Wonderland, Cinderella, etc.)
3. Place the cards in two envelopes on the bulletin board with name facing the board. Make sure that characters from the same story are in the same envelope. For example, Red Riding Hood and the Big, Bad Wolf should be in the same envelope.

USE
1. Have the students go to the board individually and take one card from each envelope. Then have them develop and write down a conversation between the two characters.
2. Pin the stories to the board for others to read.

Note: Plot, sequence, story line and length of stories may be adjusted to students maturity level.

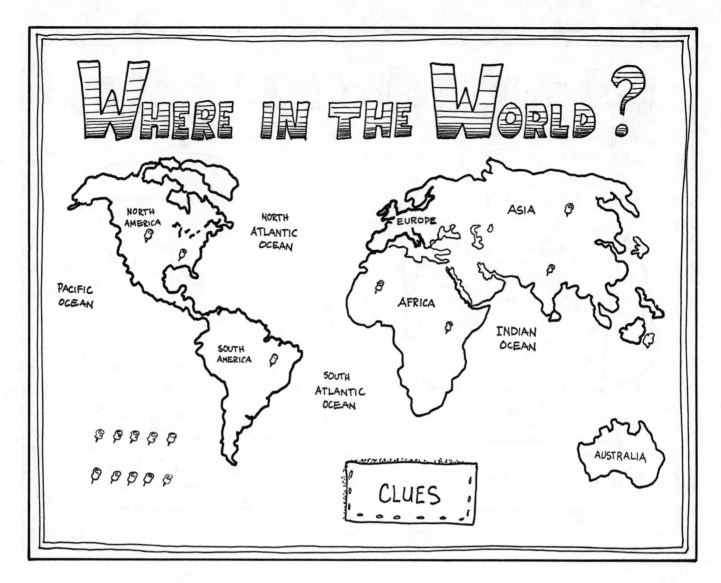

SKILL: Reading maps

CONSTRUCTION

1. Pin a large world map to the bulletin board.
2. Provide red and green push pins.
3. Make Where In The World game cards by printing one clue on each card about a place on the map. (Clues will depend on the age and maturity level of students.)
   Examples: The European country closest to Africa.
   The capitol city of Canada.
4. Pin an envelope on the board to hold the clues.
5. Divide the students into two teams. Give each team a set of colored pins.

USE

1. Taking turns, a member of each team draws a card and tries to use the clue to locate the place on the map. If successful, a pin may be placed on the spot located.
2. The game continues until all members of the team have had a chance to try. At the end of the game, all pins are counted and the team with the largest number of pins on the board wins! Clue cards may be changed to be in keeping with topics of study.

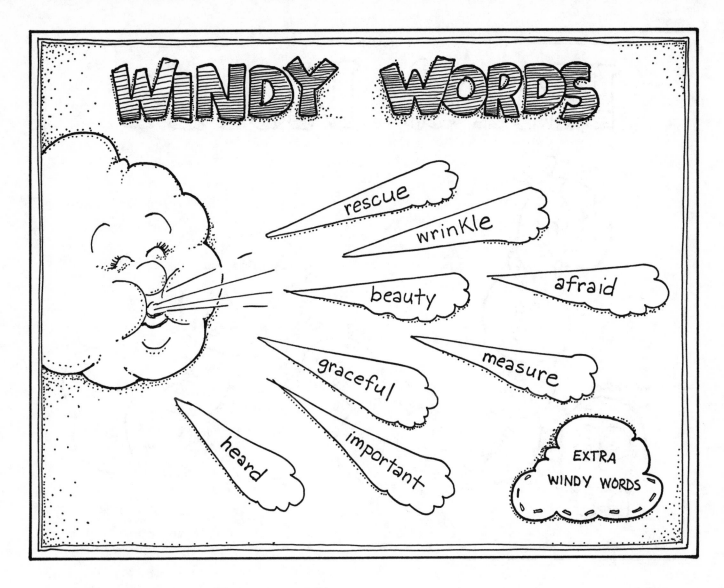

SKILL: Recognizing vocabulary words

CONSTRUCTION
1. Enlarge and reproduce the bulletin board example.
2. Cover the board with blue construction paper.
3. Make the cloud out of cotton. Make the cloud pocket out of white paper and cover it with cotton.
4. Print new vocabulary words on strips of paper and attach to the board. (These can be changed daily or weekly.)
5. Make extra words to put behind the cloud pocket.

USE
1. Introduce new vocabulary words for any subject.
2. Point to the words and ask students to say them.
3. For added reinforcement, allow pairs of students to come to the board during reading group. Tell them to practice saying the extra words in the cloud pocket to each other.

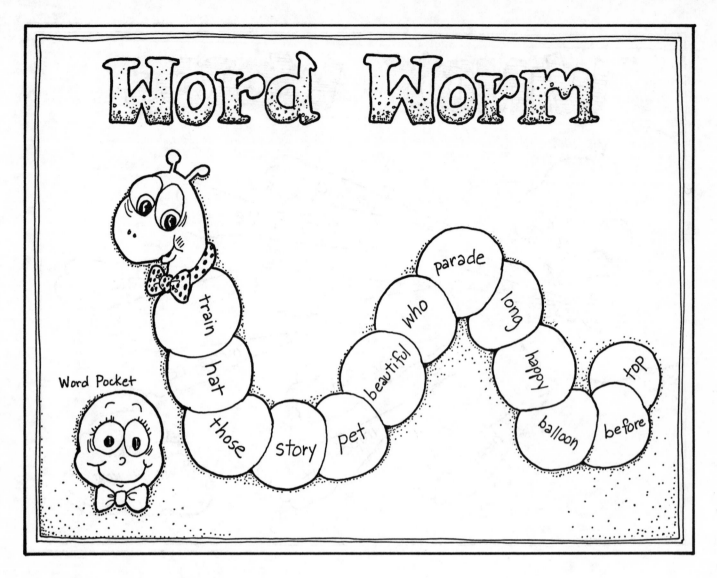

Word Worm

SKILL: Using vocabulary words

CONSTRUCTION
1. Enlarge and reproduce the bulletin board example.
2. Print vocabulary words on cards so that they can be changed daily or weekly.
3. Use green construction paper to make the worm and extra circle shapes.
4. Print more vocabulary words on the circle shapes.
5. Make a worm face, attach it to a folder and attach that to the bulletin board. Put the circles in the pocket.

USE
1. Review the sight vocabulary words on the worm.
2. Ask the class to make up sentences using the words.
3. Divide the class into two teams. Take a vocabulary word from behind the worm's head and hold it up for the first player on each team to see. The first player to pronounce the word correctly, receives one point for his team.

Optional:
Ask players to say a sentence using the word correctly. Continue the game until one team receives ten points.

BULLETIN BOARDS
INSTEAD OF
BOOK REPORTS

Sure! Why not? Book reports are excellent teaching tools but sometimes teachers and kids need something a little more exciting. Suggestions given on this page and the following pages offer some creative alternatives to the tried and true book report. Substitute one of these assignments and then use as a bulletin board display.

SUGGESTIONS:

- Ask students to write a different ending for a book.

- Have students rate the book as excellent, good, fair or poor on plot, interest, illustrations and character development.

- Tell students to write a review of the book suitable for the school paper.

- For one week, have students make a diary entry each day that a main character in the book might write.

- Ask students to write an epilogue to a book telling what might happen next.

- Have students write a telegram (limited to 20 words) to recommend the book to a friend in another city.

AROUND THE WORLD WITH BOOKS

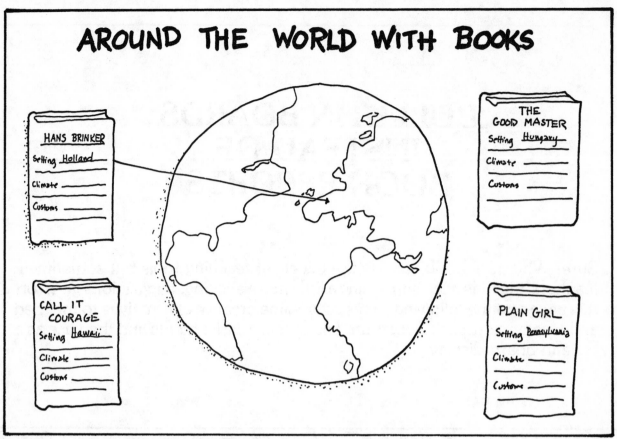

Have students mark on a world map the setting for most of a story or book. Then tell them to write a brief description of the climate, customs, etc.

Have students write paragraphs of ten sentences or less beginning with "If I had written this book..."

Have students make finger puppets from construction paper for characters in a story.

Just Hanging Around

With plastic drinking straws, thread, staples and construction paper, have students create a hanging mobile to represent the characters or events in a story.

Ring Around The Story

CHARLOTTE'S WEB

TERRIFIC PIG

Have students cut a circle from construction paper cutting out the center to make a wreath. Tell them to decorate the wreath with scenes to tell the book's story.

CHARACTER CELEBRATION

Have students plan a theme party, complete with decorations, games, menu and favors for the main characters in a book or story.

Going To Pieces

Have students illustrate a book with a torn paper collage. Remember-only glue and paper are used!

Have students design and illustrate book jackets for their favorite books.

Have students design a travel brochure describing the setting of a book.

Have students make paper doll characters for books complete with real paper doll clothes.

Have students write and illustrate 5 riddles about characters or events from the book.

Have students illustrate a T.V. commercial or write a radio spot for a book.